THE BALLAD OF RONALD REAGAN

BY

JOE JARED

FOREWARD

G. K. Chesterton's book-length ballad, *The Ballad of the White Horse*, was written to honor one of England's greatest kings, King Alfred, "because he fought for the Christian civilization against the heathen nihilism." To survey America's character today is to have the uneasy conviction that "heathen nihilism" has the upper hand at the moment. Many have a deep, desperate longing for a resurgence of "Christian civilization."

In my lifetime we have had one president, preeminent among several other great men, who served in that office with unusual courage, wisdom, faith, humility, wit, and humor. That is Ronald Reagan. So I endeavored to write a ballad about him, a partial biography in poetic form. For my primary sources, I am most indebted to Mr. Reagan's speeches and to Peggy Noonan's book, *When Character was King*.

My prayer is that another strong, righteous leader will emerge to lead the America I love out of her present decay. God grant it!

FOR THE GIPPER

DEDICATION

This paraphrase is from Reagan's speeches of February 26, 1982, March 29, 1982, December 4, 1992, and January 13, 1993.

"Presidents may come and go,
but principles remain.
To act upon the principle
makes liberty invincible
and breaks a heavy chain.

"But freedom's not from government.
It is the gift of God.
To keep it, men of faith must act
and hold, with strength and truth intact,
our freedom, bought with blood.

" 'These are the times that try men's souls,'
- the words of Thomas Paine.
For sunshine patriots can't stand,
nor summer soldiers lend a hand.
The Founders' vision for the land,
it must not be in vain."

The words of Ronald Reagan shine
as beacons in the night.
"These are the greatest days of all,
responding to a higher call
to build for liberty a wall.
This is the free man's fight.

"The sacred fire of liberty
we serve and must preserve.
For through the coldest, darkest nights
the yearning world with all its blights
looks to America's fair lights,
and hopes she will not swerve.

"For duty, honor, country we
must serve God selflessly.
America, for all oppressed,
our liberty is still the best,
religious freedom for the blessed,
bought sacrificially.

"We're here for such a time as this,
and walking with the Lord
we'll have a government for man
with rule of law for every clan
preserved by freedom's sword."

BOOK I

President Reagan began his political life as a Democrat, but left the party when he felt they were becoming blind to the error of socialism. In the 1940's and 1950's he became a member and eventually president of the Screen Actors' Guild. At that time a very real communist infiltration of several Hollywood unions occurred. The House Un-American Activities Committee (HUAC) reacted against that infiltration, and in some cases overreacted. Reagan stood courageously against both the communists (who issued a death threat to him) and against the unfair dealings of the HUAC toward some actors including even James Cagney and Humphrey Bogart.

Dutch Reagan welcomed argument.
Come all into the fray.
Freedom affords the level ground
to speak your mind to all around.
Let even anarchists resound
by public light of day.

Truth never hides itself from light.
What if a group loves guile,
pursues its power secretly,
metastasizes stealthily?
The Nazis did in Germany
until they screamed, "Sieg Heil!"

That's not American at all.
Democracy's light of day
loves not the grasping power-mad
who plot and plan with lies, stealth-clad,
and lurk in twilight's gray.

Reagan, the New Deal Democrat
loved America,
stood for collective bargaining
with justice for the struggling
and equity in law.

He joined the Screen Actors' Guild.
The unions called for strikes,
and Reagan's group opposed it,
and someone phoned a fatal threat,
but Reagan backed down not a bit,
despising commie tricks.

Though Hollywood still ridicules
the "commie infiltration,"
their work in Hollywood was real.
It never did congeal
because of honest actors' zeal
against their vile aggression.

Dutch stood against the Russian Bear
with nuanced understanding.
A House committee went too far,
blaming Bogart – so unfair,
accusing Cagney in their war,
but Reagan blocked the branding.

Cream rises to the top.
Screen Actors made him president.
A group they were, quite liberal,
and often oppositional.
This was his school of government.

To face the heads of studios:
a sticky situation.
His sense of humor stood the test,
negotiating for the best.
He ever spoke a spritely jest
to pacify emotion.

He stood against the Communists,
their work in Hollywood.
But agents in the government
blacklisted many innocent.
Against them too he stood.

In every context of his life
he tried to find the true and right
and stand for it no matter what.
Integrity cannot be bought,
nor darkness quench the light.

BOOK II

After hosting *General Electric Theater* on television and giving many talks to GE employees across the country, Reagan gradually turned toward a more conservative worldview. His public appearances earned him the label of "right wing extremist" from the usual suspects. Barry Goldwater's book, *The Conscience of a Conservative,* strongly influenced his political convictions. He accepted an invitation to be co-chairman of Goldwater's presidential campaign in California. On October 27, 1964, Reagan gave what we now know as "The Speech" in support of Goldwater's candidacy.

"I didn't leave the Democrats,
the Democrats left me,"
for even bigger government
that taxes every honest cent.
To Lenin and to Marx they bent
ever so stealthily.

Then Goldwater ran for President
and Reagan co-chaired the campaign.
A patriot's true and proper stance
must be for smaller governance
except our military lance
to block the tyrants' reign.

So Reagan spoke his famous speech
in Nineteen Sixty-Four:
"No nation can survive a tax
that breaks the honest workers' backs.
The Congress spends, and yet it lacks,
and taxes more and more.

"Do we know the Founding Fathers' gift,
the freedoms they intended?
A refugee from Cuba came,
so happy to escape that flame.
If freedom isn't here to claim,
then liberty is ended.

"Our sacred freedom is unique,
a government by people.
Can men in distant Washington
wind up your life and make it run?
Will it be better when they're done?
They act like you're a cripple.

"Shall we give up our Revolution,
America the free?
Our choice is freedom's rule of law
or the ant heap's faceless flaw,
totalitarian tooth and claw
that rules oppressively.

" 'The Constitution is outmoded,'
said Senator Fullbright.
'Our teacher is the President,
but hobbled by that document.
He must be freed to make things right.'

" 'To meet the needs of the masses,'
a senator opined,
'we must have centralized government.'
That's not what the Founders meant.
We're not 'the masses.' We're not blind.

"The Founders sought to minimize
the centralizing power
that tries to rule economies.
To do so it must grasp and seize
freedom's blood-bought flower.

"To take for the needy and give to the
greedy,
urban renewal goes on.
Can government heal all misery?
Are plans and bureaucrats the key?
Can they win war on poverty?
The tax-payer is the pawn.

"Denounce the things they want to do,
the do-good Democrats.
They'll say you're never ever 'for,'
but just 'against' the needy poor.
How many facts must they ignore
by twisting all the stats?

"We're for the Social Security goals.
'Insurance' its keepers call it,
but treat it as a tax for use.
By this deceptive, cunning ruse
billions and billions have been turned loose.
The Fund is an empty wallet.

"And what about the United Nations
where nations may seek peace?
Shall we assail our good allies
about their Third World colonies
while silent about the Soviets' lies?
Their millions in slavery increase.

"Will government reduce itself?
It never has before.
Government bureaus never die,
proliferate promiscuously,
eat up your taxes till you sigh,
and regulate galore.

"In Nineteen Thirty-Six Al Smith,
a great American,
rebuked his Democratic friends
and left them in their Marxist trends.
He walked away without amends
because they followed Stalin.

"What good is all your property,
your title or your deed
if government can bring a charge,
impose a fine, conduct a purge,
and seize your goods indeed?

"The government can make a charge,
it has the power now.
Somehow perversion has crept in,
harassed the honest businessmen.
Our freedom is endangered, then,
if righteous men allow.

"They say Goldwater's trigger-happy,
but I knew him before.
He won't send other people's sons
carelessly to carry guns
except to guard our shore.

17

"We're in a war that must be won.
Appeasement is their plan,
and 'Better Red than dead,' they say.
Should patriots give up the fray?
Are chains acceptable this day?
That's not how we began.

"Who fired the 'shot heard 'round the
world?'
Who fought at Concord Bridge?
Who stood against the Nazi blight?
Americans who chose to fight.
Allegiance was their pledge.

"Goldwater stands for 'peace through
strength.'
Appeasement is a shame.
Our rendezvous with destiny
means fighting for our liberty.
America's not tame!"

BOOK III

After hearing his speeches about
conservative values, many Californians
wanted him to run for Governor against Pat
Brown. Many citizens urged him to try. He
won by a large landslide. Using his state as
a laboratory for democracy, he discovered
that his understanding of finances really
worked, but not without strong resistance
from entrenched corruption.

He couldn't sleep at night:
to run for governor or not?
He spoke against Big Government,
proud bureaucrats and their intent,
for all that freedom means and meant,
for which our Founders fought.

The people wanted him.
At first he wasn't sure at all.
"I'm not a pol, I'm just an actor!"
The Speech became the crucial factor.
He listened to the call.

He stumped against Pat Brown
who stood for spending more and more,
considered Reagan just a novice,
cream puff not up for such an office,
to be a governor.

A long day till the polls should close
at eight o'clock that night.
He won a million-vote landslide
yet never gave himself to pride.
The people yearned for such a guide
against the taxing blight.

The day loomed foul and overcast
when Reagan was sworn in.
But Sacramento's sky was rent.
The sun leaped through an open vent.
A brilliant halo came and went
and shone on Ronald Reagan.

"I know what I believe in,
but what should I do first?"
To find some civil servants who
will work toward what's right and true
and stand against the worst.

He gave them goals and frameworks
and told them to proceed.
He shared his principles of work.
Integrity is not a quirk.
It was time to cull and weed.

Review the programs of the State
to see if they perform,
what services they may provide,
what spending may have been applied,
what wastes may cause alarm.

They found a hidden worm
in California's government.
Accounting tricks concealed the cost:
three hundred millions spent and lost,
in debt, bankrupt, and worse and worst,
still spending like a mint.

Each day new problems came to light.
The legislature schemed,
and Reagan got an ulcer then
trying to drain the frowning fen
of taxing, spending congressmen.
It was worse than he had dreamed.

One day the ulcer went away.
The Governor wondered why.
The power of prayer he knew was real.
He learned that people met to kneel
to pray for justice and for weal
that God might hover nigh.

A group from California prayed,
North Carolina too.
The medicine he set aside
and let the power of prayer abide,
encouraging and true.

For Reagan was a man of prayer,
imploring God to guide.
The State's finances turned around.
A surplus made the budget sound,
for prayer had turned the tide.

He learned negotiation well.
Like FDR he tried to bat.
He couldn't get a hit each time,
but his batting average was prime
against the Democrat.

Roosevelt's fireside chats-
he heard them as a child.
By radio and television
he made his case and shared his vision.
The liberals went wild.

Weinberger brought him news:
a hundred million bucks.
Because of tax and cutting cost
the State recovered what was lost:
a surplus in the books.

The Congressmen would surely spend it,
so Reagan acted fast.
From where it came he'd send it back
now that the books were in the black,
a rebate for the people's lack.
The Congress were aghast.

*****

To open the gates of hell,
that's what he thought abortion does.
A living human in the womb
deserves respect instead of doom.
Judges shouldn't cast such gloom
on a little face and nose.

This tragedy will end.
The child has a right to liberty,
to life and pursuit of happiness.
Raw power brought this evil stress,
all human life respected less,
debased judicially.

He wished to hear the grievances
of blacks and Mexicans.
He brought more into government
than prior governors had sent,
but only able hands.

He finished his second term
with keen welfare reform,
still caring for the truly needy,
but not deadbeats and not the greedy.
Retiring, he left things firm.

BOOK IV

Reagan's career in government brought inevitable stress. He found restoration in vigorous physical work at his ranch, the Rancho del Cielo. There he cleared trails through thick brush, getting dirt under his fingernails and sweat on his brow. He chopped wood and found himself physically strengthened and mentally relaxed. Also, riding his horse gave him a quiet space for dreaming great dreams of restoring the Founders' dream to America.

In the Santa Ynez Mountains
he had a rustic ranch.
He loved to ride his horses there,
to cleanse his mind in the mountain air,
to think about the next great dare
from which he wouldn't flinch.

Ronald Reagan's ranch:
It's where he went for toil,
for peace and solitude and sweat
to dream about what isn't yet
between the sun's rise and its set
on California's soil.

Rancho Del Cielo:
go up Refugio Road,
drive past the little lemon ranches,
the avocados' light green branches
uphill to his abode.

The Santa Ynez Mountains are
two thousand feet above
the blue Pacific to the west.
A verdant valley fills the east.
They cast a spell of strength and rest
where wholesome thoughts may rove.

When Reagan rode his horses here,
it made him think of Psalms.
"I look to the hills whence cometh my
strength,"
an open cathedral, breadth and length,
a spacious place that calms.

He thought about America,
created to be free,
a sanctuary for the brave,
who, loving freedom, crossed the wave
to build courageously.

A little house with stucco walls,
a little patio,
a longhorn steer hide on the wall,
and the horns of Duke, his favorite bull,
a humble place to go.

For Reagan was a humble man,
unpretentious, plain,
much like his house in the morning hush.
He loved to work and clear the brush,
in the early light and the sun's bright blush,
to clear a trail and a lane.

When Gorbachev first saw the ranch
he scarce believed his eyes.
Why should this powerful capitalist
abide in such a humble nest?
So Gorby went away impressed,
less bellicose, more wise.

The CBS took telescopes
to spy on Reagan's nest.
One day he grabbed his chest and fell
in pretense of a heart unwell,
and then he jumped up with a smile.
It was a clever jest.

He loved his horse, El Alamein,
and Nancy's horse, No Strings.
He loved to gallop and to trot
across the acres of his plot,
loving all nature's things.

He loved the coyote, mountain lion,
the bobcat and the bear,
the sanctity of living things,
the vista where God's beauty clings,
the sparkling leaf, the bird that sings,
the bracing mountain air.

He knew God made us in His image
and gave us the world to rule.
He thought it was sin to pollute the land
but foolish on the other hand
to comfort bugs at the expense of man.
Tree huggers can be cruel.

BOOK V

Reagan found himself in the paradoxical situation of desiring power in order to undo unbridled power. Having discovered that he could lead a great state into a better place, he gained confidence and hope that this could happen for the nation. So he put his hat in the ring to run for the office of President of the United States against the incumbent, Gerald Ford. He almost won.

Ambition was his paradox,
to seize Leviathan,
to make the bloated government
lose weight. It was too corpulent.
To tame the beast, that was his bent,
to be American.

He knew the history of man,
of freedom's fragile health,
not from enemies abroad,
but from the worms within that gnawed
and power-hungry men that clawed
by subterfuge and stealth.

The Feds did not create the states,
the states created them.
Why then is Washington a god
and not accountable? That's odd.
That's not the Founders' dream.

For money was their instrument.
They gave it to the states.
It came attached to sticky strings.
The other end to Congress clings.
The states received it though it stings
and comes with heavy weights.

Whose money was it anyway?
It didn't grow on trees.
The government bureaucracy
made rules and laws and strings, you see,
but their responsibility
was not to steal and seize.

Our Founding Fathers had foresight
to limit government:
to guard us from the enemy,
preserve our lives and liberty,
the land of the brave and the home of the
free,
just that is what they meant.

Why should a distant bureaucrat
tell farmers what to plant,
tell teachers what they ought to teach,
with arrogance and overreach
to say who can and can't?

Ronald Reagan thought these things
as he planned for days to come.
The people wanted him to fight
against the looming leftist night,
to mend the days of Nixon's blight,
to seek and overcome.

He decided he must run
against the incumbent, Ford,
but most against big government,
high taxes and the Marxist bent.
Those were the points he scored.

Don't fight fellow Republicans,
but let the public know
that "I'm outside the establishment.
To fix this mess, that's why I'm sent,
to change the status quo."

Then Reagan lost New Hampshire
by fifteen hundred votes.
In Florida he lost again.
North Carolina brought a win.
The roar of battle raised a din
in more than twenty states.

But Ford won narrowly,
and Reagan thanked his delegates.
He faced strong faces streaked with tears
and gave them hope for coming years.
"No idleness for our careers,
no rocking chair awaits.

"Never surrender your ideals,
and never compromise.
America may now be ill,
but she's a shining city still,
for millions the city on a hill.
For liberty she'll rise.

"We dreamed, we fought, and the dream
remains."
He gave a big thumbs up.
"We've lost the battle, not the war.
We're down, but we can still go far.
The only way is up."

BOOK VI

Reagan won the Republican primary in 1979. He then ran against Jimmy Carter who had referred to him as a "war-mongering nuclear cowboy." However, the nation was in distress during Carter's administration with dangerous levels of inflation and unemployment, not to mention the cold war with the U.S.S.R. and a newly adversarial Iran. Reagan was confident he could change the situation.

During Jimmy Carter's reign
misery increased.
Unemployment and inflation
escalated in the nation,
and dangers never ceased.

Carter cut the military
while communism roared.
Our forces grew more obsolete.
We faced a nuclear defeat,
an Armageddon of awful heat
by a Russian missile horde.

November, Nineteen Seventy-Nine:
Reagan for president.
He lost in Iowa outright.
The Republican primary was a sight,
but he set his face like flint.

He hit New Hampshire hard
and paid for a debate
with Bush and other hopeful men.
He wowed the crowd in the noisy din,
and he won as if by fate.

At the GOP convention
with George Bush at his side
he broke a modern precedent.
He asked them to bow and to be silent,
inviting God to preside.

He took a chance to do it,
admitting he was almost afraid,
but also afraid not to do it,
for he would need God's aid.

He hit Jimmy Carter hard:
"Recession is when your neighbor
has lost his shirt, his hope, and his job.
Depression is when *you've* lost your job,
recov'ry when Carter loses his job,
his badly misguided labor."

The Soviets were building a massive force,
invading Afghanistan,
spreading their cancer in Central America,
creating slave states in Africa.
And things were worse in Iran.

In Iran more than fifty Americans
the Ayatollah held hostage,
but Reagan couldn't stand the thought
of our decline: "That's not our lot.
We have the power to change the plot.
It's time to turn the page!"

Election Day in the afternoon
found Reagan taking a shower.
Nancy said the President
was on the phone. He dried and went.
Carter conceded like a gent,
and Reagan came into power!

But nothing ever changed him.
Whether a movie star,
a governor, or president,
his humbleness was evident.
He stayed the same wherever he went,
even when he went far.

This "war-mongering nuclear cowboy,"
(according to his foes)
came at last to Washington,
encouraging this yearning nation
with wisdom at his inauguration
to overcome our woes.

On the west side of the Capitol
the inauguration was held.
He stood beside the podium
gazing west from whence he had come
on a nation that none excelled.

He gazed at the Court's chief justice
beneath the sullen sky.
The sun burst through the clouds in its might
in a burst of warmth and yellow light.
Left hand on the Bible and raising his right,
he took the oath with joy.

Second Chronicles Seven Fourteen:
that's where he placed his hand.
"If My people, called by My name,
will turn away from their ways of shame
and seek My face, I will not blame,
but I will heal their land."

His first inaugural address
declared and declaimed
the solution is not the government.
The problem is the government.
Those who misuse the government
are elitists who must be tamed.

The result of that will be
a wider place for men
to live their lives in liberty,
to build a healthy family
in a nation of prosperity,
a place where they can win.

The White House, the Executive Mansion,
had a mystical aura for him.
He walked down the hall and suddenly
he appreciated the enormity,
the fulfillment of a dream.

Their eyes glistened with tears
as they walked through every room.
They toured the Truman Balcony,
the Oval Office prayerfully,
great symbols of our history,
the fabled Treaty Room.

America's economy
writhed in the grasp of inflation.
At twenty-one point five percent,
an interest rate incontinent,
the people suffered discontent
in the economy's gyration.

Reagan's first topic was tax reform.
He wanted to cut the rates.
With lower taxes we could grow,
create more jobs with taxes low.
More people working starts a flow
of money in the plates.

More people working pay more tax.
That compensates for cuts.
High taxes will demotivate.
Why should my hard work inflate
the government's share of my estate?
That's evil, and it hurts.

Reagan had majored in economics
at Eureka College.
He'd read Friedrich Hayek and Milton
Friedman.
He'd been a successful businessman.
Why should high taxes clobber a man
and steal from his zeal its edge?

Why bother to work overtime
if Uncle Sam will steal it?
Inflation is another thief.
It brings your bank account to grief
and makes you want to quit.

Why bother working hard and saving
when every dollar shrinks?
It makes the young live for today,
all unprepared for come what may.
That isn't wisdom's proven way.
The wise abhor such kinks.

The federal budget deficit
was eighty billion high
the day that Reagan came to serve,
but what he did took steady nerve.
He increased its upward curve
because a peril lurked nigh.

The Soviets were building bombs
at an astounding rate,
spending more by fifty percent
while our brave soldiers underwent
disrespect and hate.

Reagan met with the Joint Chiefs,
vowing to turn this around,
vowing to get good personnel
and planes that fly and ships that sail
and bombs that threaten fiery hell
where enemies abound.

He had to make a painful choice:
decrease the deficit
or make the nation safe from harm.
It's better to have a mighty arm
and show the foe our grit.

BOOK VII

An insane man named John Hinckley shot
the president nine weeks after he took office.
Hinckley wanted to be like Travis Bickle in
the movie *Taxi Driver,* shooting the
president in order to impress a pretty girl.
Another man at the scene also had been
impressed by a movie. As a boy Jerry Parr
watched a movie called *Code of the Secret
Service.* From that point forward, Parr
decided to become a Secret Service agent.
He helped save Reagan's life. Ironically the
star of *Code of the Secret Service* was a
young actor named Ronald Reagan.

The thirtieth day of March
in Nineteen Eighty-One
he gave a speech to the Construction Trades.
The talk went well with accolades
at the Hilton Washington.

He left with aides and Secret Service,
walking past the press.
"Mr. Reagan!" a reporter yelled.
At just that moment gunshots hailed
and caused a deep distress.

They pushed him into the limousine,
Ray Shattuck and Jerry Parr.
Parr told the driver, "Get us out!"
The life of our leader hung in doubt.
Six shots were fired with deadly clout
toward the big black car.

Agent Tim McCarthy fell.
James Brady also dropped.
The smell of sulfur fouled the air.
The bullets ripped a bloody tear.
Six rapid gunshots popped.

Parr pushed the president upright.
They sped to the White House.
But then he coughed some frothy blood.
His handkerchief turned red with blood,
a danger like a deadly flood
to threaten and to rouse.

He felt he couldn't get his breath.
They turned the car around
and rushed into the hospital,
and Reagan walked in straight and tall.
Knees buckling, he began to fall.
It was a sucking chest wound.

The room was bedlam right away,
trauma bay number five.
Blood pressure, heart rate faltering,
a skillful team examining
to keep the man alive.

They found no gunshot wounds on him.
Perhaps a heart attack?
He woke and then passed out again.
Someone held his hand in the din,
a reassurance through the strain,
through all the ruin and wrack.

His blood pressure was plummeting,
his lungs filling up with blood.
The bleeding must be stopped or else
the President would have no pulse.
He would be dead indeed.

They couldn't find the bullet.
They searched him, every inch.
At last they spied the entrance wound,
a bloodless little slice they found,
the site of the bullet's pinch.

Brady was shot in the temple,
Delahanty in the neck.
McCarthy became himself a shield.
Hit in the chest, he lurched and reeled.
The fourth shot struck the window shield.
The fifth was Reagan's wrack.

It tumbled and tore his muscle
and rested in his lung.
An inch from his heart, it swam in blood.
The enemy came in like a flood
and stung like the serpent's tongue.

He saw them wheel Jim Brady near
and asked for God to heal him,
and then he thought, "I can't ask God
to heal while hating the man of blood."
He asked the Lord to forgive him.

They told him he must have surgery.
That's what the doctors said.
"I hope you're all Republicans!"
"Today, we're all Republicans."
For sure they were Americans
around the President's bed.

"Honey, I forgot to duck,"
he said when he saw his wife.
Waking up in the recovery room
his optimism dispelled the gloom.
His funny notes began to bloom,
for he was full of life.

"Who's minding the store?" he asked.
"The government is normal."
"What makes you think that's reassuring?"
He had his friends and doctors laughing.
This man was presidential.

"If I had got this much attention
back there in Hollywood,
I would have stayed." That's what he wrote
with tubes in his throat as he passed a note.
His humor alone was worth the vote
for wholesomeness and good.

"There's nothing quite so exhilarating"
so Winston Churchill said,
"as to be shot at without result."
That's Reagan's reply to this lightning bolt.
Thank God, he wasn't dead.

The meanest of his enemies
sheathed their poisonous swords.
You can't be mean to a gallant man
unless you're a chump in a churlish clan.
You have to restrain your words.

Now Reagan's life would change forever.
The Lord had spared his life
to fulfill a mission as yet unknown,
to do what's right and see justice done
and not to shrink from strife.

John Hinckley's fate was shaped by a film,
but so was Jerry Parr's.
He saw the *Code of the Secret Service*
starring Ron Reagan by a roll of the dice.
He thought to become an agent was nice.
It was written in the stars.

BOOK VIII

On June 8, 1982 and shortly thereafter Reagan delivered two seminal speeches. The first he delivered to the British Parliament in the Palace of Westminster in London. It became known as the "Westminster Speech." The second was to the National Association of Evangelicals on March 8, 1983: the "Evil Empire Speech." He lifted the curtain on the Soviets' Orwellian tyranny. The usual suspects went ballistic, calling him a warmonger. Even his supporters were shocked. It's rare for a president to tell the truth with such boldness.

Truth never hides from light,
and Reagan spoke the truth.
The wardens of the gulags scowled.
The liberals sat down, appalled,
and labeled him uncouth.

On June Eight, Nineteen Eighty-Two,
Palace of Westminster,
he spoke defending free men's rights
against the communistic blights,
their gulags and their dismal nights,
the savage Soviet monster.

"We can't make the Russians worse,
but truth might make things better."
He spoke to the British Parliament
with words both wise and provident
and true down to the letter:

"Free people can work together
through economic strain.
This is my second visit here
with Mrs. Thatcher, your prime minister.
How nice to visit Great Britain.

"From here I'll go to see Berlin
and the dreadful Berlin Wall,
a fitting symbol of an evil regime,
the totalitarian terror machine.
One day it's going to fall.

"Regimes planted by bayonets
never take root to remain.
We face a threat of global war.
I needn't describe how nukes can mar,
but we can face the strain.

"The threat of global war is real,
and nukes could end mankind.
There is a threat of slavery,
of socialist bureaucracy,
police who kill in secrecy
to frighten the free man's mind.

"When World War II came to an end,
only the West had nukes.
We didn't use this awful might
to conquer nations in the night,
subduing them by threat and fright -
our argument's strong crux.

"What if the nuke monopoly
had been in Communist hands?
The world would be a different place
with little Stalins in your face
while honest men would find no grace
where evil darkness stands.

"Self-delusion is mere folly.
The West must be strong.
Totalitarian forces seek
to spread abroad their barbarous reek
upon the helpless and the weak.
Appeasement is so wrong.

"Therefore our mission is today
to keep both peace and freedom.
The Soviets deny man's dignity,
devour their peoples' liberty,
but only with great difficulty
and economic gloom.

"The size of their failure is astounding.
They spend too much on bombs.
Their economy is weak,
their peoples' daily lives are bleak,
their agriculture is a freak,
their plates reduced to crumbs.

"Of all the millions of refugees
we see in the world today,
their flight is away from the communist
sore,
never toward, but away from their shore,
far from the grim and gray.

"Today on the NATO line our troops
face east to prevent invasion.
The Soviets also face the east
to cage their people like a beast.
Their rule deserves derision.

"The arbitrary power of State
to squash individual rights
is loathed by men of dignity
like those who served at Thermopylae.
Remember the Soviet brutality
that snuffs out freedom's lights.

"Our ultimate objective then
is freedom for all men.
It's not the sole prerogative
of western men, for I believe
it is the hope of all to live
with liberty to gain.

"Therefore, we should foster this:
the light of democracy,
free press, free universities,
protection for diversities,
the right to vote for whom we please.
That is true liberty.

"The opposite is tyranny:
the propaganda of the State
instead of independent news,
no freedom of religious views,
no chance to own the land you choose,
a government you hate.

"The place for Marx and Lenin
is history's ash heap.
This has happened in the past,
that tyrannies have had their blast,
but free men tore them down at last,
for what they sow, they reap.

"Our martial strength is a necessary
prerequisite to peace.
In hope that it shall never to be used
our hearts and will must be infused
with liberty's increase.

"Britain is the cradle of self-government,
the Mother of Parliaments,
the greatest giver to mankind
of civilized ideals and mind,
where rule of law has been refined,
the people's government.

"Look back on all the perils
through which we've already passed:
the mighty foes that we've laid low,
the Nazis we have brought to woe.
Why should we fear a future blow?
Our God can quell the blast.

"For the sake of peace and justice
it's time for a new crusade
for a world that makes all people free
to have a voice in their destiny.
Never surrender liberty.
Her torch must never fade."

The Brits' applause was thunderous
for a stunning, truthful speech.
It gave our Western souls a lift
and marked a great and massive shift,
the end of a mere defensive drift.
Walk tall. Stand in the breech.

But criticism came so soon:
"Is he trying to start a war?"
But no one wants such deadly duels.
We in the West don't act like ghouls,
and the Soviets dare not be such fools.
They fear the nuclear.

"Wasn't the speech an insult to Russians?"
Reagan would smile at this.
To insult their people was not his whim.
Their government was an insult to them.
They knew too well their lives were grim
in their barbwire wilderness.

On March Eight Nineteen Eighty-Three
he called a spade a spade.
"The Marxist Leninists refuse
the precepts of religious views.
They're eager to destroy and bruise
where joys and freedoms fade.

"While in the West there is a fear
to call them what they are.
They need to know we favor peace,
but our love of freedom will not cease.
They'll see our faith in God increase.
Christ is our guiding star.

"I heard a father speak one day.
He had some little girls.
He said he'd rather see them dead
believing in the living God
than hopeless as a godless Red.
Their souls are precious pearls.

"For those who dwell in the iron jail
let's pray for their salvation,
that they may know the living God
and turn from evil back to good
that God may heal their nation.

"Until they do let's stay aware
they are the locus of evil.
In their clean, well-lighted offices
they plan their vicious practices.
It's folly to appease their vices.
Don't let your strength unravel."

The Evil Empire Speech
caused trembling in the Kremlin,
encouraged many honest zeks,
for truth turns tyrants into wrecks
and topples terrible men.

Book IX

The U.S.S.R was promoting communist
insurgencies all over the world, even in the
western hemisphere. Reagan wanted to force
them back. He wanted to help Central and
South American countries set themselves
free from poverty and to show the Soviets
that if they wanted any more of this
hemisphere, they'd have to fight for it. A
strike by the Professional Air Traffic
Controllers Organization, PATCO, caused a
national emergency. Reagan dealt with it
firmly. Foes around the world took notice of
his willingness to risk popularity in order to
do the right thing.

> The convalescing president
> faced huge complexities.
> The Soviets were burgeoning
> at South America's left wing,
> and Nicaragua felt their sting,
> who tried to grasp and seize.

But Reagan wished to help those lands
be free from poverty,
to model freedom's industry,
American economy,
to fight the Red insurgency.
Was Reagan's policy.

Mutually assured destruction (MAD)
had been the status quo.
Nobody pushed the button first
because of worse and then of worst,
the nukes to rocket and to burst,
a recipe for woe.

He was appalled by MAD.
It wasn't quite foolproof.
To foil the risk of nuclear war.
There's nothing that he wanted more.
Of war we'd had enough.

Why should we and even they
waste gold on many guns?
It was misuse of energy,
resources, creativity,
a dangerous indemnity
that stultifies and stuns.

He quoted Lenin's stated plans,
his sick morality,
to lie so long as it helped their cause,
to kill and steal by teeth and claws.
They can't be trusted to honor laws,
but they feared bravery.

They had seen our diffidence,
our weakened leadership.
The Russian bear began to growl.
In Asia it commenced to prowl.
In other continents as well
its paws reached out to rip.

But Reagan told the truth to them:
we'll never be outspent.
Our budget for defense is strong
while their expansion is all wrong.
Our free market can't be stung
by Soviet government.

He wrote a letter to Brezhnev
through strength to sue for peace.
He lifted America's grain embargo
in hope to make the arms race slow.
The commie bosses all said no.
The Cold War didn't cease.

Then something happened from within:
PATCO threatened a strike.
They wanted a big increase in pay,
a hundred percent and right away.
Eleven percent was Reagan's way,
but the union didn't like.

Reagan knew the strike was illegal
and against the public safety.
He told them he would be their friend
as long as they didn't try to bend
their contracts and the law of the land.
It became an emergency.

Seventy percent of controllers struck.
They thought Reagan was bluffing.
He gave them forty-eight hours to fold
or they'd lose their jobs and be out in the
cold.
Reagan wasn't bluffing.

This was Reagan's first great test,
a national emergency.
Throughout the world his friends and foes
watched to see how things would close.
He knew he was right; it wasn't a pose.
His strength lay in honesty.

He had a backup plan
for traffic controllers of the sky.
Non-striking workers could keep their
places
and keep the planes flying on a less busy
basis.
The union snafu caused a lot of sad faces.
A hundred percent is too high!

The deadline passed, and thirty percent
arrived to do their work.
Seventy percent called Reagan's bluff.
They lost their jobs, and that was tough.
Too late they knew he was no cream puff.
Reagan would not shirk.

The Soviets were watching him.
The commies respected power.
He was willing to be unpopular,
to stand by his word whatever the jar.
The ripples of this pulsed near and far
and helped in a crucial hour.

BOOK X

Reagan never tried to strike a pose; he was
merely himself whether relating to heads of
state or waitresses or the man in the street.
His political enemies hated him bitterly, but
he never returned the favor. He viewed
bigotry as evil, but did not favor showing
special privileges to minorities. He felt that
merit and character should be the criterion
for promotion. He had a profound respect
for women but recognized the God-given
gender differences and roles of human
beings.

The eastern seaboard fraternity -
he wasn't in their club.
His voice was for the common man.
They felt that he was in their clan,
that he would never snub.

Reagan was an actor
yet never insincere.
No one could call him phony then
and make it stick through thick and thin.
Integrity was Reagan's kin
throughout his long career.

An honest man in Washington
makes enemies too soon.
They called him unsophisticated,
stupid, lazy, addlepated,
senile, cornball, antiquated,
an affable buffoon.

They called him mad and warlike,
a bomber and a bore,
an incoherent cretin dolt,
a dim bulb shy of watt and volt,
a Strangelove, less or more.

But who was truly wrong?
Truly time would tell.
For Reagan had imagination
to see the past of a mighty nation
and bend it in a new direction,
a new but old as well.

Our history was never a blind fate
that sweeps us all along
like lemmings rushing off a cliff,
but rather great men who live their belief
can sing a great new song.

Reagan thought that people are smart,
inventive and creative.
In Hollywood he had seen
the genius of the American scene
and ingenuity so keen
where people work and live.

For America is the place
where genius is allowed,
where you can work and earn your pay
and spend it in whatever way.
Because of freedom, it's okay
just as the Founders vowed.

They called him an evil idiot.
That hurt, but he didn't lose sleep.
He had faced opposition in Hollywood.
The commies had threatened to shed his
blood,
but he stood his ground in that bitter feud
though its bitterness was deep.

It helped that he knew he was right,
defending America's muse,
rewarding creativity,
laughing at arrogant enmity,
the talking heads in the news.

He didn't hold resentment
against his enemies.
Though Donaldson had tried to damn,
he merely said, "Oh, that's just Sam."
He never harbored hatred's flame,
and he didn't bend in the breeze.

Most politicians create an image
of what they want people to see.
But Reagan was merely who he was.
He never tried to take a pose,
a man of integrity.

What did he think about race?
Everyone equal in the eyes of God
and equal in the laws of men.
Don't judge by the color of a man's skin
but only character. Amen.
The quota system is flawed.

What did he think about women?
In Hollywood women were strong,
respected, smart, and able to lead,
able in thought and able in deed.
Respect for women was in his creed.
He learned it when he was young.

He thought of women as equal to men,
but he didn't think they were men.
He thought they were even better than we,
longing to civilize humanity
with wisdom, tenderness, and charity.
But he didn't see them as men.

He respected Margaret Thatcher
and knew Jeane Kirkpatrick was wise.
She knew the nature of evil states,
totalitarian reprobates,
dictators and their arrogant traits.
He picked her to advise.

Reagan loved his parents:
"When my mother died I thought
I would never, ever smile again,
but after a while you do smile again.
She taught me that bigotry is a sin,
unjust, and an ugly blot."

He never forgot a friend.
From Dixon, Eureka, Rock River,
from Hollywood and Washington,
the illustrious and the unknown.
For him to keep in touch was fun.
He loved his friends forever.

Book XI

Reagan dealt with crisis upon crisis during his administration. Two of these were arguably the biggest. The first was the problem of freeing American hostages unjustly held in the Middle East. Among these was a CIA station chief, William Buckley, an American patriot, held by the pro-Iranian terrorist group, Hezbollah. After meeting with the families of these innocent Americans, Reagan's own heart ached to free them from the despicable people who held them. The second, and arguably the greatest crisis had to do with the Soviet Union and the escalating Cold War.

> The golden crown sits heavy
> on the brows of kings.
> They face pressures we don't know,
> the presidents who come and go
> as troubles follow to and fro,
> fortune's arrows and slings.

He had crises right away,
in the days of communism,
their Latin American insurgencies,
their shooting down from Asian skies
a Korean airliner to its demise
in heartless atheism.

Reagan fought the tax and spend
mania of Congressmen
with battles of budget and battles of tax.
For liberty he fought the liberal hacks.
Big taxes are a sin.

He dealt with war in Lebanon,
the bombing of Beirut,
of barracks full of our Marines,
of our embassy by evil schemes,
Islamic terror's terrible means
to murder and to loot.

The commies invaded Grenada,
and Reagan kicked them out
to save our students who studied there.
How good it was to have one less lair
of slavery in this hemisphere
because our defense was stout.

The Philippines were falling apart,
and the *Challenger* exploded.
They killed the Egyptian President
whose work for peace was evident.
The terror-makers ripped a rent,
and ayatollahs gloated.

One crisis in particular
hurt more than all of them.
The Iran-Contra gave his foes
the stick they wanted to rain their blows.
They clamored like a flock of crows
as they closed in on him.

And this is how it came about.
Hezbollah, the "party of God"
was torturing American hostages
taken from Beirut in cages.
Reagan was angered by such sacrileges
and wished to do what he could.

He was told that Israeli contacts
had connections in Iran.
The ayatollah was said to be sick.
A moderate government could be the next
pick.
Negotiations might do the trick,
and that became their plan.

Reagan thought it was worth a try.
He let the talks begin.
Iran wanted some antitank weapons
for opening the hostage dens
to free our suffering men.

Israel would sell them the weapons,
but we would replace their supply.
Reagan opposed this deal at first,
trading with thugs, the worst of the worst,
but Mossad wanted to try.

Mossad, the Israeli intelligence
was held in high regard.
The president wanted our hostages free.
They made the shipment secretly.
One hostage came home presently,
freed from the prison yard.

Reagan waited for more to be freed,
but the Mideast exploded again.
Israel bombed the PLO.
Islamic Jihad struck back with a blow.
They killed Agent Buckley, our man.

After they claimed to have killed him
four terrorists hijacked a ship.
They shot a helpless, disabled man,
a wheelchair-bound American
and threw him into the Mediterranean,
a heartless, cowardly step.

Fifty American tourists
aboard the *Achille Lauro*
Reagan determined to protect.
The hijackers sailed to Egypt direct.
The U.S. sent SEALs to intersect
those men of the PLO.

We learned that the men would be flown to
Tunisia
aboard an Egyptian plane.
American fighter planes forced them to land
in Sicily with a powerful hand.
Our SEALs rushed the runway, arrested the
band.
Alas, it was in vain.

For Italy refused extradition
and took custody on their own.
At least they were caught and would be
tried.
They tried to run, but they couldn't hide.
Justice tracked them down.

Shultz warned the President not to pursue
the arms-for-hostages deal.
It wasn't really technically that,
but surely it would look like that
if leaks should begin to reveal.

But Reagan wanted our people released
because of his hope and compassion.
He thought he was dealing with moderates
who could open Hezbollah's dismal gates
and free our folk from terrorist states.
That was the President's mission.

In the meantime terror spewed death again.
Qaddafi fomented it.
Libyan ships attacked our fleet,
but American warriors brought the heat,
and Qaddafi took a hit.

Libyan agents bombed a disco,
hurting our servicemen.
Reagan would deal with this mad clown.
He brought Qaddafi's headquarters down.
In smoke and flame the work was done,
destroying the tyrant's den

Qaddafi took revenge.
He paid ransom to Hezbollah
for one of the hostages to kill.
He killed him with devilish hate and skill.
Was this the will of Allah?

The Catholic priest, Father Jenco,
the terrorists released.
So Reagan had hope for the rest of them,
but Weinberger thought the hope was dim.
Treacherous is the Mideast.

Reagan would not give up.
A newspaper printed the tale:
we traded arms for hostages.
Congress had hearings and rants and rages,
but the President weathered the gale.

The scandal blew sky high,
and people called for impeachment.
Congress had hearings, investigations,
talks, grand juries, and jubilations
while hopes for our men in their captivations
faded and failed and went.

Later Reagan said he was wrong.
He should have listened to Schultz.
He tried to explain it to the press,
but most would rather curse than bless.
So, they hurled their bolts.

One weekend Meese reported
that Lieutenant Colonel North
diverted a part of Iranian gold
to Nicaragua, so it was told,
to help the freedom fighters hold,
for freedom has great worth.

And some resigned and North was fired
and Reagan addressed the nation.
He gave the people the history
and shed light on the mystery
and called for investigation.

He waived executive privilege
to bring everything to light.
The Iran-Contra escapade
ended at last with Shultz's aid.
He answered hard questions and didn't
evade
till the scandal faded from sight.

Reagan gave Schultz authority
for dealing with Iran.
The thing that most hurt the President
wasn't a scandal that came and went,
but rather Americans, innocent,
imprisoned in Iran.

All those involved in Iran-Contra
paid a very high price.
Some lost their jobs, and some were fined.
Some were embarrassed and left behind,
an adverse roll of the dice.

The opposition found a chance
which they never had before.
Ben Bradley of the *Washington Post*
said since Watergate this was the most
fun he'd had to scorch and roast.
The Dems let out a roar.

Eager to capitalize,
they televised their hearings.
Lieutenant Colonel Oliver North
they tried to grill for all they were worth.
Instead, he grilled them back and forth.
While stinging they took some stings.

Best of all for freedom
the Sandanistas fell.
A prodemocracy government
in Nicaragua pitched their tent.
The commies came, but the commies went.
Democracy worked well.

Nevertheless for Reagan
it was a terrible loss.
But Nancy helped him to laugh again,
and comforted him with her gracious mien.
A bigger crisis loomed on the scene
with bigger dice to toss.

BOOK XII

President Reagan chafed at the mad idea of mutually assured destruction (MAD). That was the only thing preventing a surprise Soviet nuclear attack on America. They knew we could retaliate. Yet Reagan knew that man had never developed a weapon he had not, sooner or later, used in war. So he had the idea for free American ingenuity to build a shield, missiles that could knock out incoming missiles before they spewed their deadly radiation. This idea, strangely, was derided by the usual suspects. History has a different perspective.

Ideas have consequences
that make or unmake lives.
Marx and Lenin had their dream.
Their man-made heaven didn't seem
quite what it truly was, a scream
where bloodshed coils and thrives.

The Twentieth Century
was different than before,
for war had targeted the weak,
rending children in its beak,
killing women in its reek.
The devil lurked at the door.

Man had never made a weapon
that he failed to use.
After Hiroshima's burn
what prevented another turn?
That was Reagan's great concern,
to cut the terrible fuse.

Women and children had always died,
the innocents in war.
But nuclear bombs could wipe away
a country in a single day.
Millions of people could decay
inside one burning hour.

Reagan wanted a missile defense
to stop incoming nukes.
The joint chiefs thought it could be done.
He told them to take the plan and run
and make a shield by brain and brawn
to foil the communist crooks.

Strategic Defense Initiative-
the press derided it.
They thought it was very entertaining,
useful for Reagan's further defaming.
Star Wars they called it, foolishly blaming
a highly creative wit.

Think, therefore, of this:
a hundred thousand bombs.
Later or sooner brimstone will spew.
The threatened country will launch one or
two.
What's left of mankind will be few
when Armageddon comes.

In July, Nineteen Seventy-Nine,
Reagan had gone to NORAD,
the Aerospace Defense Command,
the place where nuke defense is manned.
Even that would fail to stand
against an atomic prod.

Mutually Assured Destruction (MAD)
was not what Reagan would choose.
Therefore he charged the Chiefs of Staff
to take no measures merely half.
We had too much to lose.

A hundred fifty million souls
would die in a nuclear war
even if America won.
This grisly fact could only stun
the earth like a falling star.

Reagan shared his dream with the nation.
You'd think the world would love it.
But, no, the press, the talking heads,
the Soviets and all the reds,
the Democrats with all their dreads
had a collective fit.

They said it was impossible,
but Reagan was a man
who wished to save ten million lives,
to kill those missiles in their dives,
to send their stings back to their hives,
to bring about their ban.

They said it was too expensive,
but Reagan said, "Think again.
How valuable is a single soul,
and what if ten million is the toll,
and what if they kill your kin?"

They said it wasn't needed.
"MAD has worked so far.
We've treaties with many, outlawing the
nukes."
But treaties get broken by dirty crooks.
How many treaties are in the books
as yet unbroken by war?

They said it would destabilize
and prompt a Soviet attack.
But Reagan said MAD was still in place.
Besides, we would share SDI by grace.
The world could sleep better in such a case.
The future would not be black.

The Soviets were furious
because it threatened their power.
They were treated with respect and fear
because the great red Russian bear
had power to scorch the very air
within a single hour.

Their leaders resisted for another reason.
They believed in American brilliance.
They feared we could make the *Star Wars*
work.
They tried it themselves in stealth and murk,
but they couldn't dance such a dance.

Some of the brightest of Russian minds
languished in prison cells,
doing hard labor and suffering.
The workers' paradise had a sting
and gulags and prisons and hells.

Reagan told the Soviets
he wanted serious talks.
He wanted genuine arms reductions,
not merely little limitations,
to cull the nukes by powerful motions
and cut them down like stalks.

For years there was no breakthrough.
Brezhnev and Andropov:
death came to them and laid them low
and did likewise with Chernenko,
and then came Gorbachev.

Warm words would not change Soviets.
We didn't share their views.
One thing alone could change their tune.
It's strength alone dismays a goon
and gives a bully a bruise.

Therefore, we built our great armed forces.
We launched our ships of war.
We made more guns of tempered steel
and fielded men of martial zeal
to bring the Soviets to feel
our might, both near and far.

The Russian arms were burgeoning,
amazing in scale and cost,
their long-range missiles too many to count,
they bristled with rockets and tanks to
mount
a great attack on the weak and the gaunt.
They were a frightful host.

But Reagan's strategy worked.
Their missiles aimed at the west.
Reagan ordered them taken down
or we would bring Pershing II's to town
aimed at sovereign Soviet ground.
He didn't do this in jest.

The Soviets didn't back down.
We deployed our Pershing II's.
The peaceniks whined across the West.
They called Mr. Reagan a warmonger, a
pest,
but time would prove his plan was the best.
The Russians had much to lose.

They blinked and came to the table.
"Gorby has a nice smile,"
it was said, "but also iron teeth."
He didn't look like warmed-over death,
a man of wit and wile.

They first met in Geneva
in a bitterly cold November.
SDI was Gorby's preoccupation,
abhorrent to his communist nation.
They were against it on every occasion.
It burned them like an ember.

Gorby could not believe
we'd share SDI with them.
He thought it would help us to strike Russia
first,
to finish them off in a fiery burst,
but Reagan said peace is America's thirst.
We find the arms race grim.

Gorby had vigor and cleverness.
He made no territorial claims
for San Francisco's Russian Hill.
He had humor and an iron will,
but on his heart was the wish to kill
our SDI and its aims.

Reagan said SDI is better
than a race for arms.
He said it's a race that you can't win,
and World War III would be a sin.
Why can't we come to agree again,
to bring an end to harms?

Geneva was a good beginning.
The leaders exchanged their letters.
At last the Soviets agreed
reduction of nukes was a true need,
but one thing surely America must heed:
on *Star Wars* put some fetters.

If so, the Soviets
would stop their nuclear tests,
and by the end of the century
both sides could end the atomic fury,
but forego the *Star Wars* quests.

But Reagan foresaw some roadblocks.
What about nuts with nukes?
What if Qaddafi or another freak
got rockets with nukes? That thought is
bleak.
For defense SDI is still unique,
a shield against the crooks.

Meanwhile the Russian economy
was cratering day by day.
They couldn't afford their enormous arms
race.
Reagan knew he must keep his pace,
hold his ground, and stay.

The Russians arrested an American,
and Reagan was mad as hell.
Gorbachev wanted further talks,
but Reagan said, "Not till Daniloff walks,"
and the Russians opened their jail.

They agreed to talks in Reykjavik.
There a great crisis occurred.
Gorby wanted to talk about arms,
but Reagan wished first to talk about harms
and human rights and third world alarms
in which the Soviets erred.

However, they talked about arms reductions.
Gorby said breathtaking things.
They would do away with bomber planes,
ballistic missiles and all such banes
and allow inspections in all their plains,
and that without any strings.

They even agreed to reduce their forces
east of the iron curtain.
They would reduce their troops and tanks,
diminish their presence, ranks upon ranks,
of that we could be certain.

It all depended on one little thing:
get rid of SDI!
Reagan couldn't believe his ears.
They'd already talked about such fears.
The Russians could come and inspect the
gears
of the dreaded SDI.

If it looked like *Star Wars* would work,
the Russians could take it home.
Both sides could deploy it at the same time,
and Gorby had thought the idea was prime.
It could be an invisible dome.

But now at the end of their summit talks,
Gorby went back to square one.
Reagan knew through intelligence
the Russians were working on their defense,
their own *Star Wars*, an aerial fence,
an SDI all their own.

Gorby just wanted to kill SDI,
destroy it once and for all.
Reagan sat back with a frown and a look.
"The meeting is over!" That's all it took.
He stood up and left the hall.

In Nineteen Hundred Eighty-Seven,
a chill lay twixt us and them.
But on June 12, a great event,
up to the Berlin Wall he went,
perceiving what that grim symbol meant.
Its evil angered him.

He spoke to Gorby across the Wall:
"If you truly seek
openness and liberty,
Eastern Europe's prosperity,
tear down this Wall of tyranny,
a wall that imprisons the weak."

Reagan's face showed anger
against that bleak empire,
its prisons and its gray gulags
where humans were treated worse than dogs
behind the sharp barbwire.

Four months later Gorby came.
He caved on SDI.
All the intermediate nukes
were banned according to the books.
Inspectors peeked in all the nooks
to "trust, but verify."

If Reagan had taken the deal
offered at Reykjavik,
it would have been a great breakthrough,
a coup undreamed of, out of the blue,
but he was a patriot through and through
who wouldn't leave us weak.

Because he refused at Reykjavik,
the Soviet Union fell.
They couldn't keep up with the USA.
The rest of the world was no longer their
prey,
and all the mapmakers had a heyday
redrawing all their lines.

They shipped out to America
a six-ton piece of the Wall.
The last stop on its itinerary
happened to be the Reagan library,
a monument of its fall.

BOOK XIII

This paraphrase is from a part of Reagan's
farewell speech to the nation.

After eight years in the White House
he wasn't preoccupied
with writing his personal legacy
or spinning his recent history.
He retired satisfied.

He prayed before his farewell address.
"My fellow Americans,
back in the early Nineteen-Eighties
the boat people chose not to live on their
knees.
In leaky boats they set sail on the seas
to live in freer lands.

"Our aircraft carrier *Midway*
patrolled the South China Sea,
rescuing those who fled Vietnam,
who wished not to live in the socialists'
frame,
who loved only liberty.

"Our sailors spied a rickety ship
all crammed with refugees.
They sent a small launch to tow the boat,
to make doubly sure that it stayed afloat
as it pitched on the choppy seas.

"A man in the boat saw a sailor on deck.
He stood up and called to him,
'Hello American sailor!' he said,
'Hello freedom man!' No dread
of tyranny would vex again his head.
He had dreamed the American dream.

"It was a small drama, but huge with hope.
We stood again for freedom.
Our long recession had come to an end.
Our values and virtues were on the mend,
our heritage from Christendom.

"They called me the 'Great Communicator,'
but it wasn't my words or style.
I talked about America's heart,
the truths we held from the very start,
the wisdom our Founders had to impart
through tribulation and trial.

"They called it the Reagan revolution,
but for me it always seemed
a great rediscovery of common sense.
We found that old values had power to
cleanse -
the dreams our ancestors dreamed.

"Because we are great, our challenges are
too.
It will always be that way.
As long as we hold to the principle,
America will be invincible.
That's the prayer I pray.

"To preserve the Constitution,
to bring 'We the People' back.
The rule of law must be observed;
separation of powers must be preserved
to put us on the right track.

"I spoke of the shining city
my entire political life,
and here's what I saw – a tall, proud place
built on the rock of God's great grace,
teeming with people who dwell in peace,
where trade and commerce are rife.

"And how is she now, America,
two centuries since she began?
She's holding her own in storms and wind.
She's still a beacon and still a friend
to pilgrims from places that fail to defend
the justice and rights of man.

"We weren't just marking time.
We made a difference.
We made the shining city strong.
We made her freer; we fought the wrong.
God bless America's freedom song
for all the ages hence."

EPILOGUE

This paraphrase is from Reagan's comments
on May 6, 1983.

"Standing up for America
means standing up for God,
for God has greatly blessed this land.
The Ten Commandments came from His
hand.
They aren't suggestions, but command.
To love Him isn't odd.

"He wants us to love our righteous Lord,
to love our neighbors too.
If we do this well, we'll solve our woes,
climb our mountains, defeat our foes.
Who knows what we might do?

"The United States remains the last,
the best hope for mankind
plagued by tyranny and want,
oppressed by enemies that haunt
with wickedness of mind.

"Well, I believe in you,
and if we work together,
then one day we may truly say,
'We fought the good fight as well as we
may,
we finished the race and didn't delay
till evening shadows gather.'

"Then to our children we may say,
and to our children's children,
'we did everything that we could do
to make the world much better for you
in our brief time beneath the blue,
the sky and the risen sun.'"

BIBLIOGRAPHY

Ronald Reagan, The Wisdom and Humor of the Great Communicator, Edited by J. Ryan, Jr., Copyright 1995 by the Ronald Reagan Presidential Foundation, Collins Publishers San Francisco, 1160 Battery Street, San Francisco, CA 94111.

Peggy Noonan, *When Character Was King,* Viking, Published by the Penguin Group, Penguin Putnam Inc. 375 Hudson Street, New York. New York, 10014 U.S.A., Copyright Peggy Noonan, 2001.

Dinesh D'Souza, *Ronald Reagan,* Touchstone, Rockefeller Center, 1230 Avenue of the Americas, New York, New York, 10020, Copyright 1997 by Dinesh D'Souza.

Barry Goldwater, *The Conscience of a Conservative*, Hillman Books, New York, Victor Publishing Company, Inc., 1960.

G. K. Chesterton, *The Ballad of the White Horse,* Dover Publications, Inc., Mineola, New York, 2010.

24876523R00060

Made in the USA
San Bernardino, CA
09 October 2015